YOU CAN SEE GOD IN THE WIND

Darleen Modisette

Inspirational Press
P O Box 100
Colmesneil, Texas 75938

Email: InspirationalPress@gmail.com

Website: www.InspirationalPress.net

Photography by Darleen Modisette

Edited by Miranda Darleen Allen

ISBN: 978-0-9840833-0-5

Printing by Falcon Books
San Ramon, California

PRINTED IN THE UNITED STATES OF AMERICA

FOREWORD

As author of this book, I would like to recommend that you determine to read and reread the story of Muddy's life. His story is meant to be a life guide. It is formatted and written in the very most simplistic way ever presented in a book of any form of encouraging advice literature .

This book's main objective is to illustrate how you can become all that you can be, by simply using the wisdom of the ancients as well as today's wisdom. This wisdom of which I speak is that of learning from the mistakes of others, rather than repeating the same mistakes in your own life, suffering the same consequences needlessly. The definition of insanity is "doing the same thing over and over expecting different results".

I believe the story to be timeless as well as ageless. By timeless, I mean that the book revolves around profound truths that are as old as time. To some, these truths will be greatly enlightening. To others, they will be a simple review of how life really works and how to go about being successful in any endeavor they undertake to do.

By ageless, I mean no one is too young to learn from it, as well as no one is too old to learn from it. My most sincere desire is to enlighten the novice or very young readers, or listeners for that matter. Also, I wish to inform the young as well as the older reader who may have never known or may have forgotten this wisdom and subsequently made choices that carried some very harsh consequences along with that decision.

After teaching this type of wisdom over the past twelve years in the Texas Prison System, I can truthfully say: All the wisdom of which I speak, can be condensed down into the main storyline of the book you now hold in your hands. No matter what your age, you will find that this is truly the way to successful living, simply put into story form.

The story is rather short, yet precise. At first reading, it will probably not convey it's very deepest of truths to you. However, on the second, third, or perhaps even the fourth reading, the hidden wisdom will become more evident. This is why I recommend multiple readings.

Also, I recommend future readings every time you feel your life is spiraling out of control. Every time you embark on a new career, a new adventure, a new endeavor, or a new relationship it would be wise to remember the simple advice here. To do so will make a real difference in your life.

The first reading provides the entertainment of a good story. Seeing someone finally reach happiness and success, even though he is just a lowly, helpless creature in the beginning, is uplifting and encouraging. For after all, aren't we all just the same? Aren't we all helpless, lowly creatures at birth in our most humble beginning?

Some may have more opportunities than others. But, each time anyone implements the wisdom mentioned in this book, that person is granted that which is much more valuable than any opportunity could ever afford. He or she is rewarded with inner peace, strength, power and all the advantages of the ONE that they followed to that success.

The second reading provokes a little more thought as you follow Muddy's life and compare it to your own. After all, we are all born with the same tabula rasa or blank slate. At birth, no one gets anymore brains or wisdom than anyone else. We truly are all created equal; with no knowledge whatsoever.

The third reading provides the crown of considerate thought. As you place yourself into the situation, according to where you are in your personal life, you begin to see logically. Putting ourselves in someone else's place always helps us to see ourselves more clearly.

The final reading is where you begin to refer to and implement Muddy's discoveries into you own situation. Behave like Muddy and achieve the success of your dreams. Remember, "I can do all things through Christ Jesus who strengthens me". Philippians 4:13. Happy readings!

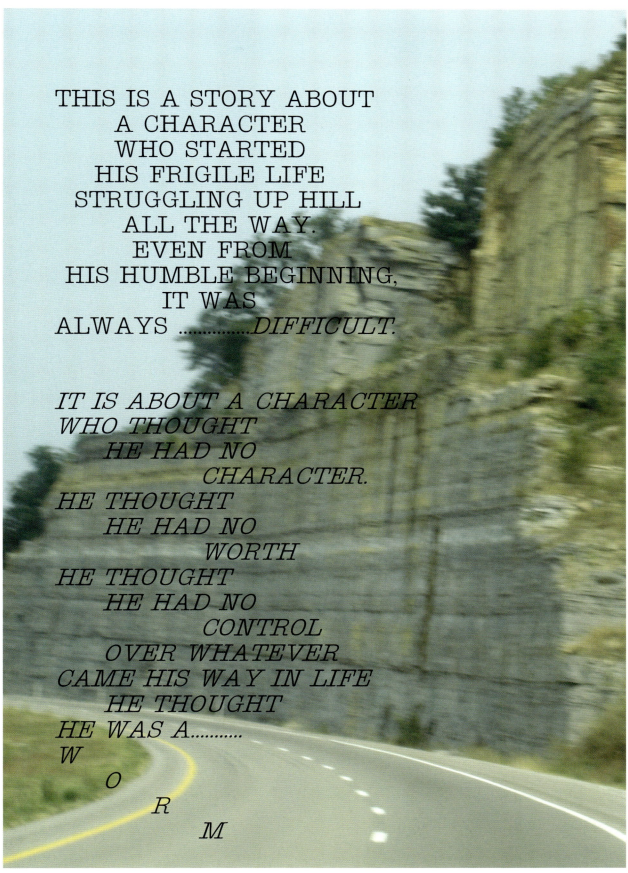

THIS IS A STORY ABOUT
A CHARACTER
WHO STARTED
HIS FRIGILE LIFE
STRUGGLING UP HILL
ALL THE WAY.
EVEN FROM
HIS HUMBLE BEGINNING,
IT WAS
ALWAYS ....DIFFICULT.

IT IS ABOUT A CHARACTER
WHO THOUGHT
HE HAD NO
CHARACTER.
HE THOUGHT
HE HAD NO
WORTH
HE THOUGHT
HE HAD NO
CONTROL
OVER WHATEVER
CAME HIS WAY IN LIFE
HE THOUGHT
HE WAS A...........
W
O
R
M

Now, maybe Muddy thought he was a worm because somebody **told** him he was a worm.

Maybe, he thought he was a worm because some-one **called** him a worm.

Maybe, he thought he was a worm because they **told** him his **Father was a worm.**

Or, maybe it was simply because he was a...

W

O

R

M

Reflection

Have you ever been called names?

Names mean nothing, unless you take ownership of that name.

When you are called a name, don't get angry...just consider the source.

Try to realize the name caller's motive. Are they trying to bully you?

Try to discover the why, and the wherefore will become apparent.

When looking deeper, you will find the truth. Is that person angry?

Why are they angry? What's the true source of their anger?

Answer these questions and you will find their true motivation for their

negative behavior.

Saint Francis of Assisi said, "May I always seek to understand before I seek

to be understood.".

When you try and finally understand truly why you are being called ugly

names, you neutralize any influence those negative words may have

held over you.

Name calling is always an extension of the caller's own deepest fears

about his own self image. Because he feels powerless concerning himself, he

turns to trying to push someone else further beneath his low status.

Never call anyone names, lest you be revealed to be the very thing that

you despise. Keep your words sweet, you may have to eat them.

MUDDY WASN'T AN ORDINARY WORM. HE WAS A WORM WITH GREAT POTENTIAL AND A VERY SPECIAL CHARM THAT HE KNEW NOTHING ABOUT.

BUT, THAT DIDN'T MATTER BECAUSE, HE THOUGHT HE WAS JUST A PLAIN, COMMON, EVERYDAY, WORTHLESS WORM.

HIS SELF-WORTH WAS LOW AND HIS IDEA OF WHAT LIFE WAS ALL ABOUT WAS RATHER FUZZY.

JUST LIKE THE PICTURE HE SAW OF HIMSELF IN THE MIRROR, HIS SELF-IMAGE WAS BLURRY. IT EVEN SHOWED IN HIS PHOTOS; KIND OF LIKE THE ONE ON THIS PAGE: IT WAS OUT OF FOCUS.

Everywhere ... ... muddy most of the tim... ... ... to be muddy. It seemed ... ... just one big

MUDDY RIVER

The only thing Muddy hated more than mud was the wind.

The wind was his biggest enemy.

Everytime the wind blew, dust and dirt covered Muddy.

Then he would have to shake and shake himself, to get up out of the dirt so he could walk on top instead of under it.

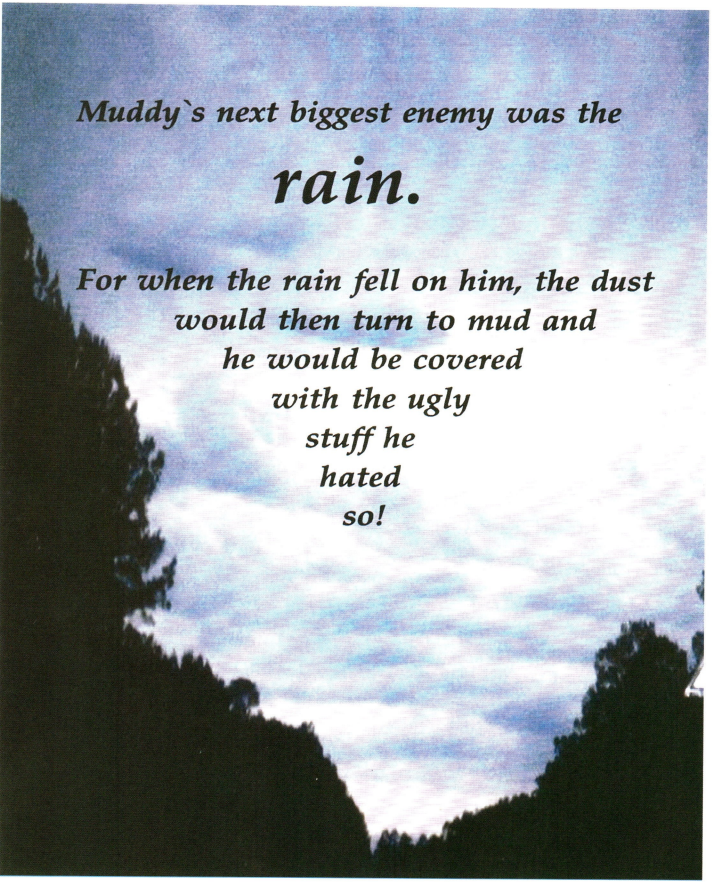

Muddy's next biggest enemy was the

rain.

For when the rain fell on him, the dust
would then turn to mud and
he would be covered
with the ugly
stuff he
hated
so!

Once in a while the day would be beautiful and Muddy was able to walk proud. But, all too soon, the wind would come again. And, he'd be covered with the dust that he knew would soon turn to mud.

"Oh, how I wish I could change", Muddy cried.

"Why, oh why can't I change?"

So, Muddy did try to change. He
changed the way he walked, he changed the
way he talked. He tried to walk high on his
tiptoes, which didn't help. The wind
just blew harder.

Then , the rain returned and finished
the job.

Once again, Muddy was.........Muddy!!!

Over and over again!

MUDDY GREW OLDER AND DECLARED "I AM WISER

NOW. I WILL DEFEAT THE WIND AND RAIN. I WILL

RISE ABOVE THE DIRT. I WILL ONLY GO OUT IF

THERE IS NO WIND AND THERE IS NO RAIN.

Muddy stayed inside for the longest time, because the wind blew continually. Soon, Muddy was very hungry, but, the cupboard was bare.

Poor Muddy

Had nothing to eat.

He was....
        Starving.

Once again, he gave up and decided to return to the outdoors.

Once again, he was defeated by the wind.

Once again, he was covered by

Mud..

Muddy looked up and saw a church. It made him hopeful.

"Oh, how I wish I could change", Muddy sighed.

He closed his eyes and prayed.

"Please, please, I want so much to change."

JUST AS MUDDY FINISHED HIS
PRAYER, A BEAUTIFUL BUTTERFLY FLEW
DOWN BESIDE HIM; AND WHISPERED EVER
SO SOFTLY, IN A HAUNTINGLY SOLEMN BUT
REASSURING VOICE, AS SOFT AS A SMALL
SUMMER BREEZE,

"YOU MUST FIRST KNOW WHAT YOU WANT TO
CHANGE INTOOOOOO.....THEN DO.....
WHATEVER IT TAKES
TO CHANGE".

Just as the butterfly floated away on the breeze, Muddy called after him.

"I do, I do. I want to be like you. Before I die and my life is through, I want to be just like you"

The words came from someone Muddy could not see but,
Surely could hear.

"Then find one of your kind,
One just a little older, a little wiser than you.
Follow every move they make. And, do whatever
they do.
Do whatever it takes to become
A whole new you.
Someone you can be proud of."

The words seemed to follow Muddy
Could this be some of that ancient wisdom
Muddy had sought after in his dreams?

Could this be the **secret** to life?

Could this be the answer to all his problems?
Maybe, just maybe, he would be able to find
The happiness he had longed for, for so long.

Maybe this **was** the answer he had searched for!

So, Muddy set out to do what he must do.

He found the "special one" in a flowering bush. He followed him for a few days and then he discovered him high in a tree.

Muddy watched as he began to spin a shell around his feet.

"Why,, that is so senseless", Muddy pondered........
"Now you can't walk"

BY FAITH I DO WHAT I MUST DO.

FOR, AS I TRAVEL THIS ROAD, I KNOW IN MY HEART,

I WILL NOT STAY LIKE YOU."

AFFIRMED *THE ONE.*

MUDDY KNEW IF HE KEPT DOING WHAT HE HAD BEEN DOING, HE'D KEEP GETTING WHAT HE HAD BEEN GETTING. NOTHING WOULD EVER CHANGE.

BUT, HOW COULD HE EVER LIVE WITHOUT HIS FEET?

THEN HE WATCHED AS THE 'ONE' SPINNED MORE AND MORE. THE 'ONE' COVERED HIMSELF COMPLETELY, ALL THE WAY TO THE TOP OF HIS HEAD. HE HAD EVEN COVERED HIS EYES.

"OH, BUT I NEED MY EYES!" MUDDY CRIED. "I **REALLY, REALLY** LOVE MY EYES".

THEN, IT SUDDENLY DAWNED ON HIM. "IF I REALLY WANT TO CHANGE, I MUST BE WILLING TO DO WHATEVER IT TAKES." **NOW**, HE FINALLY UNDER-STOOD THAT UNLESS HE CHANGED COMPLETELY, EVEN HIS EYES AND THE WAY HE SAW THINGS, EVEN HIS MIND AND THE WAY HE THOUGHT THINGS; HE WOULD NEVER CHANGE ANYTHING. HE WOULD STAY FOREVER A MUDDY, LITTLE, FUZZY, UGLY, **WORM**.

IMMEDIATELY, MUDDY BEGAN TO SPIN, AND SPIN AND SPIN. AS HE SPUN HE SANG THIS LITTLE SONG.

FIRST, YOU MUST KNOW WHAT YOU WANT TO CHANGE INTO.......

THEN FOLLOW OLDER AND WISER ONES WHO'VE GONE BEFORE YOU.

NEVER LOOK BACK, NEVER COUNT THE COST,

NEVER COMPLAIN ABOUT, WHAT YOU THINK YOU LOST.

JUST SPIN THROUGH FAITH AND SPIN THROUGH HOPE

TRUST IN CHRIST JESUS, TO ALWAYS HELP YOU COPE.

KNOW THAT EVERY GOAL IS GETTING CLOSER FROM AFAR.

AWAY FROM WHAT YOU WERE AND INTO WHAT YOU TRULY **ARE!**

AS MUDDY SANG, IT GREW DARK AND SOON HE WAS FAST ASLEEP.

Early in the morning, Muddy stirred. It seemed like it was the very next day to Muddy. He stretched and yawned and then began to push and shove and bite and scratch until he was loose from his tomb.

He pulled himself out and looked around. Just as he did, he realized that he had forgotten how high up he was and he began to.............

Fall

"Oh, no," Muddy thought. "I'm done for now!
As he fell, he struggled and flailed around and began to

F LY!

Then he began to drift slowly on the wind. He
Dipped and swirled and soared.
He breathed in the sweet orange blossoms that were all
Around him. As he floated, he realized the wind is now...

My friend. I will never be Muddy again!

Muddy looked down where he was flying over the water.
There he saw his reflection and what he had become.
It was the most graceful butterfly he had ever seen.

He had become a beautiful *butterfly* just like he had dreamed about.

"Come on Buddy. Fly high with me." said the softest, sweetest voice Buddy had ever heard. *"The wind is great today!"*, she called.
Without a thought, Buddy flew off to catch up with her.

Now, Buddy knew he had made the right choice
"I'll never be muddy again." he declared.

*"I'll **never, ever** be muddy again."*

About the author:

I was born of Christian parents who were, I believe, chosen by God himself, to be my "special ones" to follow. Though my career is very different from theirs, my life's purpose is exactly the same. Two sisters, Wilda and Dean spoil me to this day.

My dad, Hugh Keith, was a "giver" as was my mother, Bonnie Hock Keith. They both followed the Cherokee way of being peace loving, generous, and gracious with everything they had. Not only our Cherokee ancestry, but the Scottish, English, Irish, also, were known for their kindness and willingness to help others less fortunate.

Funny thing about it, most folks would think we were the ones who needed the charity. We didn't have, but we didn't know we didn't have. My parents counted their blessings and found that God was more gracious to us than we ever deserved. We had very little sickness in the family and never bad accidents that could destroy families. Aunties, uncles and cousins galore. We loved each other. And we still do to this day.

I was not only blessed with a wonderful family, I was born into a great "Church Family", in Pt. Arthur, Texas, at Calvary Baptist Church. Through this church's nurturing I found life more abundant and free through Jesus Christ.

I continued the traditions of my family with my own beautiful children who now have beautiful children of their own. My oldest daughter, Melinda, with her husband, Mark, and daughter, Miranda are now wonderful neighbors and a great Christian family. My son is our Hero, three times off to foreign wars, leaving wife, Colleen and six children to protect others. Clint is also the brains of the clan, as he is first to begin work on his doctorate degree in technology. They're also a great Christian family.

My youngest daughter is my birthday present extraordinaire. She and I share our birthday each year. Vicki is the caring angel I wish to be. She and her family serve God as well as serving country. Her husband, Matt, is in the military. Both daughters named their daughters after me, Martha and Darleen which I consider an honor of the highest degree. It's been my pleasure to carry both my grandmother's names as my first name. To tell how great my nine grandkids are will take another book, and eons of time. Corey and JA among seven granddaughters, poor guys.

My best friend is and always has been my dearest cousin, Donna Dean Hock Hatton. We've been mistaken for twin sisters, which thrills us both to no end. Thanks, Donna for your encouragement to go ahead and publish <u>You can see God in the wind</u>. Had it not been for you convincing me that the cover photo phenomenon was a sign from God, I may not have had the courage to do so.

Saving the best for last, I tell you of Tom, my wonderful husband. He is my genius, counselor, guide, confidant, provider, protector, defender, friend, and lover. He is a wonderful step dad to my kids and grandkids. God gave him to me, cause he wanted to bless me abundantly. Life is good, God is great, and beauty is everywhere, if we will just raise our eyes and lift up our heads.

DEDICATION

This, my first attempt at writing a book, is dedicated to all the students who have passed through my classes over the past fourteen years. From the encouragement of that first 1996 sixth grade class in Malakoff, Texas, to the fourth grade class in Woodville, to the encouragement from students in Goodman Prison in Jasper, Texas, I have gleaned awesome wisdom.

I thank you because I have always learned more from my students than any college class or other studies I have undertaken. My life has been richer and more successful because of my time with my students. I never met a student I did not love and learn from. My current students, although they are adult men, are no less encouraging than the children. Without these spectacular men's encouraging words, I could not have accomplished this work.

Actually, the enthusiastic concern, inspirational motivation and persistence of my students pushing me on to publish is why you now hold this "dedicated to better lives" book in your hands. I appreciate all the faith you have in me accomplishing my goals.

I also want to give a special thank you to my students, Curtis Dale Stowell and Leonardo Jimenez for asking me almost every day "Did you get your book published yet?" over and over again. When Mr. Stowell graduated my classes, last fall, Mr. Jimenez took up the baton, and like a relay runner, he continued the chant. Just yesterday, Mr. Stowell came by to say hello and let me know he was using what he learned in class to stay out of trouble. However, the first words he spoke were, "have you published your book yet?". It was this kind of prodding that kept me going after the disappointment of hitting the proverbial brick wall many times.

Last, but certainly not least, I want to thank my wonderful husband Tom. Tom is my Rock. I am married to a wonderful genius who makes me believe anything is possible when you have faith. My fantastic children, Clint, Melinda, and Vicki and their spouses always inspire me to follow my dreams, as I watch them accomplish theirs, while raising my nine wonderful grandkids. My sisters, Delores and Wilda have always spoiled me, while bossing me, telling me what to do. I'm so glad they told me to publish. They gave me rave reviews when reading the book and made me believe what I constantly teach my students to say, namely "With God's help I can do this". Thank you. I am eternally grateful to you all.

Advice to my Grandchildren

To my nine wonderful Grandchildren:

My greatest joy is my family. My greatest happiness is that each one of us has committed our lives to someone greater than ourselves. Each of us has dedicated our lives to Jesus Christ, whose face appeared on this book's cover in the center of the windmill, inspiring my choice of names for the book.

To you, my darling grandchildren. Miranda, J.A., Mattie, Corey, Janice, Courtney, Brooke, Cammie, and Macey: I leave this legacy and counsel.

"In all thy ways acknowledge him and he shall direct thy paths," is a powerful Proverb's promise. For greater direction read Proverbs chapter three.

Follow this guide and you will be all that you were born to be. Your life's purpose will not go unfinished. Live by this and you will be greatly successful in both your physical life and in your Spiritual life as well.

Remember the greatest _gift_ is Love, whether you are giving it or receiving it.

The greatest _sacrifice_ is Love, whether it is given for you, or you are giving it for someone else.

The greatest _happiness_ is Love, whether it is yours or someone other than yourself

The greatest _success_ is determined by Love.

The greatest _dream_ is for Love.

And all this is accomplished through Love.

Live in this way of instruction from God to ensure your happiness.
Teach your children these ways to ensure their happiness.